Original Monologues and Scenes For Teens

by KeriAnne Dawson

Monologues & Scenes Acting For Teens

First paperback edition February 2026

Cover design: by Crosby Mowry

ISBN 979-8-218-89289-0 (paperback)

Dedicated to ~

My mom Crystal, my stepdad Tommy, Aunt Mary, my dad Tony, my amazing husband Jerry, and my beautiful children; Bradianne and Crosby.

They are my truest inspirations.

Also, a special thank you to Scot and Angela.

Table of Contents

DRAMATIC

THE AUDITION ROOM

I was in the audition room getting ready for my big cold read when, all of a sudden, I felt this big wave of heat moving across my body. I couldn't breathe and thought, *this is it. I'm not going to make it out alive.* I stood there frozen for what seemed like an eternity. I knew everyone could see me sweating; the fear – man, the fear was overwhelming. The lights in the room were dimmed, except for a bright spotlight shining down over me, it was hard to see anyone; they were practically sitting in the dark, but I could feel all eyes on me. I was looking around, trying to play it cool, but all I could do was plan my escape. Then I heard this calming voice from a dark corner say, "you got this." I don't know what happened, but my spirit suddenly felt lifted, and my anxiety left the room. I took a deep breath and just went for it. I found out later that it was one of the casting agents that spoke those words to me, which I will always be grateful for. Because I ended up nailing my audition, and I – well – I got the part.

COMEDY

NATURAL ACTING ABILITY

I've heard so much about your acting classes. My mom's friend told me that you are one of the best acting coaches in the city, so I had to come in and see for myself. I've never had acting lessons before but feel like I have a natural ability to be one of the greatest. I woke up really early this morning – the sun wasn't even out yet – and as I was sitting up in my bed, I started thinking about my life, and that's when it hit me: I want to act. I really believe that with your help and hard work, I could one day have my own star on the Hollywood Walk of Fame. I know I'm a bit of a dreamer, but what's life without dreams, right? I can laugh, I can cry, and get angry all in one short scene if the role called for it; I feel like I would make a great actor. I'm so glad to be here. I look forward to learning all I can in your class.

COMEDY

MEXIAN FOOD

I love Mexican food. The only problem is it doesn't like me back. The bean dip is not very friendly after about an hour, you know what I mean? It's pretty embarrassing. I said to my date, if this is any indication on how things are going to end up with our future, we're doomed! When its Mexican night or Taco Tuesday, I'm a complete gassy mess! I'll even order a kids burrito just so I don't overeat, and it still happens. I can't catch a break. It's quite possible I'm going to develop PTSD from this one dinner outing. I can see the big picture. I'm sitting at the table eating dinner, someone throws out a joke, and I laugh hysterically and before you know it, I'm needing to make a run for the border and quickly. I'm definitely thinking pizza next time. It's got to be a safer bet.

COMEDY

NO-SEE-UMS

I hung out with my grandmother recently. The first night I was there, she thought it would be a great idea to eat our dinner outside by the pool, and it was a great idea, for about a minute. Once we were outside, I found myself waving my hands all over my face, neck, arms, and legs; I looked like a crazy person. I told my grandmother that something was biting me, but I didn't see anything. She laughed and said, 'Oh, those are just no-see-ums.' I was like, 'Oh, they can see me, but I can't see them!' She said, 'They must love your sweet blood.' In the meantime, I was still being eaten alive by these invisible piranhas. I looked at my grandmother and noticed that she wasn't swatting any parts of her body. I asked her, 'how come they're not biting you, grandma?' She said, 'Oh, they don't like my skin lotion.' I was like, 'Grandma, I need your lotion! I'm getting attacked out here.' Anyway, I am happy to report that I'm marked safe from Grandma's house. As you can see, the lotion definitely worked, so all is good!

COMEDY

EARWAX REMOVAL KIT

My mom bought me an earwax kit because she said that I don't hear so well anymore. She thinks I could've developed some wax build up over the years, and now that I'm older, she's concerned that it's gotten worse. I did notice the other day, when she asked me to clean my room, how it didn't register with my hearing; then the same thing happened yesterday when she asked me to do the dishes. My mom said she's pretty convinced that I have a lot of wax build up in both my ears, and that it could be impairing my auditory perception. I even questioned myself: *Could this really be true?* Maybe she's right. All I could think about was how I'm too young to have hearing problems. As I was opening the earwax kit, my mom walked in laughing. It was at that moment I realized that she didn't really believe that it was a wax issue at all; she was only joking with me. She is convinced that I have selective hearing because when she says the word 'clean,' I shut down. I'm glad to know that my hearing is A-OK, but my selective hearing may need some attention.

COMEDY

OLD DOG, NEW TRICKS

I was trying to teach my dog Charlie new tricks the other day, but he insists on doing the same ones over and over again. The thing is, he knows how to sit, shake, roll over and walk across the floor, but he doesn't seem to know how to catch treats in his mouth. If I throw a treat in the air, he just stares at me, completely unfazed, and waits for it to land on the floor; then he goes after it. It's frustrating because I know he can do it; he's just being lazy. He looks at me as if I'm being unreasonable for making him work so hard for such a small piece of food. He's smart, he knows it's only for my personal amusement, and he's not having it. I don't know who's teaching who here!

DRAMATIC

ABSENT FATHER

Your dad is the best – don't ever take him for granted. Mine was never around when I was growing up, and he never paid child support. My mom worked really hard to support us. It wasn't easy; there were a lot of struggles, especially financially. It's OK, it happens. You know, my Mom did everything on her own, and although she barely made ends meet at times, she did it and I'm proud of her. She never asked anyone for anything. My mom just knew that she had to provide for us. What I don't understand is why my dad never once called to wish me a happy birthday over the years. I was a loving little girl; did I not deserve a phone call? I was told that he was really young when I was born and didn't know how to be anyone's parent, so here I am, living my life without him. I do wonder if he will ever regret living without me. I feel blessed that I have a loving family that are always there for me. I don't know what I would do without them. When I see kids at school talking about how their parents are always in their business and how they can't stand it, I just shake my head and say to myself, if only they knew what it was like to have one of them missing, maybe they wouldn't wish for such things. Sometimes it's hard to miss what I never had, but when I see others with both of their parents, I feel something deep inside and it hurts a little, but I'm OK.

COMEDY

COMPUTER CRASH

I woke up this morning and tried to turn on my computer, and it didn't work. I can't figure out what's wrong with it. The thing is, I don't even care about my documents or anything like that; I just want to save all of my photos. All I know is, if I have to buy a new one, I'm going to be so bummed out. I'm trying to save up for a new car, and this will definitely set me back by a whole year, at least. I'm really hoping that the Nerd Squad can fix it. I have about 10,000 photos to get back, and once I do, I'm going to print them all out. Well, okay – maybe not all of them, but most of them. No, I'm going to have them all printed.

COMEDY

STUPID SMARTPHONE

Every time I talk into my phone, my words turn out to be completely different; it's an embarrassment. As I was sitting in my car at a red light, I started texting my boss to let her know I was running a few minutes late for work. This internship means so much to me, but the humiliation came when I didn't have time to proof-read before pressing send. My boss got the text, and it did not read the way it was supposed to. Apparently, what I thought I sent and what she read, did not match up whatsoever. What I thought I texted was, Hi Barb, sorry I'm running late, stuck in traffic, be there soon. What Barb read was, Hi Boob, sorry I'm running away, strange traffic, barfing soon. When I walked into the restaurant, everyone was looking at me as if I had three eyeballs and a sign on my shirt that read, "Text much?" I just blame my smartphone for always proving to me just how dumb it really is. Funny enough, my boss thanked me for starting her day off with some "laugh out loud" humor. She even went on to say that she hopes I'm late again, so she gets another interesting text. I smiled and walked away. It's nice to know that there are still people in this world with a sense of humor. Although amusing, I think I'll just call next time.

DRAMATIC

DON'T GIVE UP

You mean you have a chance to be happy like you've dreamed about, and you're sitting here pouting because you didn't get that one acting role out of many? Think of all the possibilities you can have, if you never give up! You just have to take it one day at a time, you'll see. Look how beautiful your smile is; you literally light up a room everywhere you go. You have just as much of a chance as anyone else. You've got this as long as you don't give up. The time is right here, right now – this is your golden opportunity. Everything you've ever dreamed about can actually come true if you just have faith and believe in yourself. I know you have another audition today at two o clock, so what are you waiting for? Get going, and good luck!

COMEDY

IT'S ONLY ALLERGIES

Why is it when someone coughs or sneezes, people look at you like you just gave them the worst flu cooties? Before you say anything – I'm not sick; it's just my allergies acting up. I know I didn't have them at the beginning of the year, but it's a different season now, so my allergies are on 11. I promise it's not what you think. I mean, I'm not sure what you're thinking, but I can assure you that you're not going to catch anything from me. My allergies aren't contagious. On the off chance that you do wake up sick in the morning, it's not from me – like I said, it's only allergies.

DRAMATIC

COFFEE SICKNESS

How do so many people drink coffee first thing in the morning? I feel sick drinking just a few sips; it has an adverse effect on me. I end up feeling jittery right before I break out into a cold sweat. One morning on exam day, I drank one tiny cup of coffee – I even put some milk in it, you know, to give it a calming effect. The next thing I knew, I turned into a zombie. I had the most difficult time focusing; my eyes were in a trance. My hands were clammy, and my stomach was queasy. I sat there frozen in time, just staring at my test paper for what seemed like an eternity. Once I saw the other students leaving, I noticed that I hadn't answered one question, so I panicked and started checking random boxes. The next day, my teacher handed out our test papers, and right when I was going to tell her about my coffee experience, she laid my paper down and said, "Congratulations, you made an A!" I don't know how that happened. I mean, how lucky can one person be? Either I have unforeseen magical powers, or the coffee made a part of my brain super smart.

DRAMATIC

THE REAL WORLD

Who says we have to leave home when we turn 18? Where is the rule book on this? I'm not in a big hurry to leave the nest – at least not right now. I see my friends already struggling to pay their bills; they're always asking their parents for money to help with groceries or a car payment. It's crazy. I noticed the other day that a gallon of milk and a box of cereal together is about $11. Some people barely make that in one hour at their jobs; I would know – I'm one of them. I just need to focus on college and save money so I can invest in my own place one day. Plus, I don't mind getting home-cooked meals while I'm still in school. I just want to be prepared for the real world after college without the financial struggle. You know? Everything is already hard enough. I can't rush a good thing; I'll know when the time is right.

DRAMATIC

NAIL SALON PARANOIA

One of my best friends went to Stylish Nails Salon in the mall four days ago and ended up getting a staph infection. Apparently, it was from one of the employees not cleaning the foot tub properly. I feel so bad for her. I mean, honestly, how hard is it to do your own nails? I know a lot of people that want to feel pampered for a day but think about how many feet have been sitting in that same tub just minutes before the next person arrived. They stay busy. Don't get me wrong, there are some really amazing nail salons out there, but this one had a low rating on their window. My friend said she only paid $10 dollars for her pedicure; hello, big red flag right there! I don't know any mani-pedi salons that would touch your hands or feet for $10 dollars, it's unfortunate. My friend is on antibiotics and says she's never going back to another nail salon again. I can't say that I blame her.

DRAMATIC

DRIVING TEST NERVES

I am so nervous about my upcoming driving test. I mean, what if I just freeze when the driving instructor asks me to parallel park? I'm going to sweat so hard; I just know it. It's definitely going to be noticeable when I'm wiping my sweaty palms all over my pants. What if my hands get so clammy that they slip right off the steering wheel? I'm going to be a complete mess. There's got to be a better way to take a driving test these days. I know, what about a virtual test? Everything is virtual now. The DMV can just assess everything from their location, then simply let me know if I passed or not. That would be the modern way; unfortunately, by the time they figure it all out, I'll be too old to drive. I'll just keep practicing in this abandoned grocery store parking lot, until test day. Wish me luck!

COMEDY

MEXICAN FOOD FOR BREAKFAST

Gross, that's awful! What did you eat? There is no excuse for this. That is off the chart; you need to make a doctor appointment for this one. Why would you eat Mexican food right before class? Hasn't anyone ever showed you what real breakfast looks like? I mean, don't you eat eggs or pancakes like normal people? Beans will do you in every time; everyone knows this. That is just nasty, dude. Cut it out. Seriously, if you do that again, you're going to have to run home for a change of clothes. I'm willing to bank on it. Look, whatever you've got going on here, it's about to be an unpleasant situation for you – for all of us. It's a good thing no one's here yet. From a friend to a friend: Why don't you go home? Take something for this gas problem you're having, and maybe take another shower. You know, start the day over again. I'll see you in about an hour. Go!

DRAMATIC

WE CAN DO MORE TOGETHER

I know your pain more than you know, and I'm here for you. We have to get your life out of 'pause mode.' It's time to stand up to the one person who has beat you down for all of these years: you. Your story is true and real; I can empathize with you. I'm a firm believer that once you have the right people on your team, miracles will start to happen. I know you don't like talking about any of these things, but it's not good to hold it all in, either. It only builds up enormous stress. You have all the support from me. Just know that we can do more together than alone in this life; it's time to climb mountains and make things happen. Let's do this!

COMEDY

PIMPLE BEFORE HOMECOMING

It's the same sad story I've been hearing from you for weeks. Why don't you just go ahead and get some cream or something for your pimple so you can finally get rid of it? I know your embarrassed, and I'm sorry that it feels so frustrating right now. But honestly? No one is paying as much attention to it as you are. You're still a teen, you wouldn't be human if you didn't have at least one or two. Do you really think that people aren't going to give you a second look if you have a pimple? It's what's behind that pimple that truly matters. The person that you are is much greater than a red blemish on your face. I understand how you feel, I get them all the time too. Look, I'm not going to lie, yours is colossal, but I'm your best friend I can tell you these things. The good news is, it's not permanent. But if it were me, I would have already zapped it. So, before it turns into a planet, let's go to the store and grab some cream so we can get to homecoming.

DRAMATIC

I DON'T LIKE YOU FOR YOUR CAR

You know, we talk to one another on the phone every day, and it's really great, but I feel like I'm in a relationship with only my phone. It's weird. I know you don't have a car, but we're young. It's no big deal if our parents have to drop off and pick us up sometimes; it's nothing to be embarrassed about. Driving is overrated anyway. Plus, I don't like you for your car. I mean, having a car is nice, but it's you I want to see and hang out with. Oh yeah, I don't expect you to pay for everything either. I have my own money to pay for half of everything. We're teenagers it's not like we have our adult jobs yet, so if you're comfortable with it, my mom said she can drop us off at the movies and pick us up when it's over.

COMEDY

THE AUDITION

Today, I auditioned for a film called The Darkest Water. As soon as the Director yelled "action," a tall dark monster started chasing me into this big pool. I couldn't see anything. The water was pitch black, and that's when it happened. I peed. I peed in the pool. It's like my body didn't know the difference between real and make-believe – because once that monster started chasing me, I got really scared. I had this expression of humiliation all over my face when I walked out of the pool; it's as if everyone knew what I had just done, but thank God they didn't. I believe the director thought my acting was pretty good; he could see the look on my face was pretty genuine. I guess it all worked out in my favor because I think I'm being considered for the role. The only problem is this whole jump-scare thing is overwhelming. My bladder can testify to that! But if I take the role, the crew will probably have to hire a pool cleaner just in case I accidentally do it again. But what am I complaining about? This would be a role of a lifetime.

COMEDY

COMFORT FOOD

It's no secret that I have a lot of stress these days. I mean, it feels like the world is going absolutely bananas, and honestly, a banana sounds pretty good right about now. Lately, people all around me have something to complain about, including myself. If there were an island for just complainers, it would sink. The truth is, I don't always want to care about everything, but I do, and that's when I start reaching for comfort foods. The ugly truth about me and food: we're super compatible, it's overwhelming, but we just fit. You know, I've learned that there's food for every occasion and emotion. When I'm sad, it's chocolate chip cookies dipped in milk – then I'm good. I don't typically eat when I'm mad, but I think about it. The worst one is when I'm bored; that's the hardest. No matter what I'm doing, it's snack time again. I should weigh 300 pounds right now; thank God for genetics and a fast metabolism because this is not OK. I'm what you would call a 'kitchen rat,' but in human form. I worry about everything, and when I worry, eating makes me feel better. It's crazy, I know. Is there still pizza in that box?

DRAMATIC

MY SOLO

I finally started a new band with some of the best musicians I could find. We all share a mutual respect for one another and keep our boundaries in check. But when we played a big outdoor show at school last week, it made me question the mutual respect thing. The crowd was energetic and lively, and for a moment, nothing could go wrong – or so I thought. During one of our songs, I went to take my solo and noticed everyone in the audience looking passed me. For a second, I thought maybe they couldn't see me, but I knew they could since the spotlight was shining down on me. I turned around to see what the crowd was fixated on and noticed that two of my bandmates were still playing their instruments during my solo. I later realized they were unsure of what to do on stage and resorted to awkward, improvised noise that brought negative attention to us. I seriously considered quitting that night, but they punished themselves enough by ruining the song. I'm confident it won't happen again.

DRAMATIC

GAS MONEY

I finally bought my new jeep that I've been wanting. It only took me two years to save up for it, and now, it's finally mine. I gave every penny I had to buy it. The only problem now is gas is outrageous. I now have the car of my dreams, and inflation happens. I've been asking my family, what's going on. All I can think about is how difficult it's going to be to get back and forth to school every week with the cost of fuel. Filling up my gas tank is more than an average allowance in a week! Before you know it, we'll be living life similar to *The Little House On The Prairie*, riding around on a horse and cart while every modern car becomes extinct and sitting in a city dump somewhere. I just want things to be normal again. I've already filled up twice this week; I'm going to need a Flintstone's car and strong feet if I'm going to survive this.

DRAMATIC

CHEWING GUM

I don't know what the big deal is; it's just chewing gum. Why does my teacher always make it feel like it's a crime to chew gum in class? She's always asking, "Would you mind spitting out your gum please?" If only some teachers knew just how boring some of their classes really are, then maybe, just maybe, they would lighten up on a little chewing gum. My thoughts on this are simple: If the class were more exciting, maybe I wouldn't need gum to help me stay awake. Chewing helps me feel like I'm doing something productive. It's gum! It's not like I'm eating pizza in the classroom – not that I wouldn't do that, because I totally would – but gum? I mean, seriously, it shouldn't be a big deal. It's just a comfort thing to help me feel more alive in the moment. First period is such a sleeper.

COMEDY

HOUSE SLIPPERS

Last month, we bought a new puppy. We figured it was time to give our dog, Charlie, a new playmate. The thing is: our new puppy loves to steal everyone's house slippers, but not to chew on. She likes to snuggle with them, and now we have no slippers and have to wear our socks around the house if we want to keep our feet warm. When we try to take her slippers away, she just lies on the floor and starts whimpering. She's so spoiled, so we all give in and hand her back the slippers. I don't know if this is normal, but it's definitely adorable. We've tried buying her soft squeaky toys, ropes to play tug-of-war, big smelly bones that only a dog would love, but nothing works. Give her a fluffy slipper and off she goes. Can you guess what we ended up naming her? Cinderella, what else?

DRAMATIC

IT'S ONLY MONDAY

It seems like everyone around me is always complaining that it's Monday. It's like they've decided that Monday is doomsday before it even begins, and I totally get it. I even feel this way sometimes. It's the start of a long week for work and school, and everyone has to get up early. It's no secret that Mondays have such a bad rep, but I feel like we've trained ourselves to feel this way. It's kind of dumb, because it's the Mondays that make us appreciate Fridays and Saturdays. It's all about perspective. So, for me, I look at it like Mondays are a fresh start–a clean slate. Everyone should welcome that. I say let's get back to appreciating every day that we have on this earth and start celebrating that.

COMEDY

WATER BOTTLE FLIPS

A few of my friends asked if I wanted to have some fun bottle flipping, but it didn't sound like a fun time to me at all. But somehow, they talked me into it, so I did it. I have to admit, it wasn't that bad! You get a water bottle that's halfway filled with water, then you begin flipping it until it lands sitting straight up. If it falls over, you get to go again – it's two out of three. I know it sounds stupid because I thought the same thing, but somehow, I found myself being the loudest and the most competitive flipper in the house. It was definitely an adrenaline rush, and I was shamefully hooked. It's really a mindless piece of entertainment that could have kept me busy all day, but I knew if I didn't end it soon, my whole day would've amounted to absolutely nothing. So, I took the bottle and drank the water. It was game over!

DRAMATIC

SOCIAL MEDIA

Every time I get on social media, 'people you may know' pops up, and I find myself scrolling through a whole list of new faces – ones that are mostly friends with other people that 'you may know,' and even then, you barely know them! I'm not trying to befriend the entire universe; I just want to reach out to family and friends, since some of them live far away. We all know it's a great way to stay connected to one another, but it's getting ridiculous now, like nothing is private anymore. Social media shouldn't be this overwhelming. I don't need to know the whole world, and I don't need them knowing me either. My family taught me about stranger danger at a very young age. I mean, these are things you just never forget. So why are we inviting people from all over the world to be our friends? Have we all gone mad? If you really think about it, you don't really know these people, and you're letting them into your whole world – it's kind of scary. Nothing is private anymore, and I value my privacy.

DRAMATIC

FIREPIT ON THE BEACH

I was at the beach last night with some of my friends, and everything was going great until the smoke from our firepit started making everyone sick. The wind got a little crazy and caused embers to start flying around. My friend who was sitting next to me got one in her eye and started screaming. People were rushing over, thinking someone was getting attacked. I mean, I can see why they thought that, since we were splashing her in the face with water from our bottles – it was a scene right out of a movie! She was cold, wet and crying, but she's good now; at least her eye is going to be OK. Needless to say, the night was a complete disaster. We all agreed that next time we hang out, we are definitely doing a living room camp-out. Blankets, snacks, and movies all night.

DRAMATIC

COOKIE DOUGH

Every year our school sells cookie dough to raise money for band. I get that we need new instruments and all, but I'm just not a cookie dough salesperson. I mean how does that even work? 'Hi, I'm so and so from band. Please buy our frozen cookie dough so we can buy new instruments for our school.' I mean, wouldn't it just be easier to ask for money? I personally don't feel comfortable asking people to buy desserts that I won't even eat myself. The thing is, I really love cookies – just not *these* cookies. I'm not saying they're bad; they're just not good. I've even thought about quitting band so I don't have to sell foods that have ingredients I can't even pronounce. Maybe I'll just ask the band director if I could sell magazines instead. I mean, it's definitely a lot healthier.

DRAMATIC

CALL BACK

I wish casting agents could take one look at my picture and say, 'yup there's my next big star!' I just don't understand why auditions have to be so intimidating, especially when I've spent my whole life auditioning – Ok, not my whole life, but you know what I mean. Shouldn't I be immune to these kinds of things by now? I was in the casting room getting ready for my first scene, when all of a sudden, my stomach started getting queasy. I felt like I was going to throw up; my mind was just racing. That's when I knew I had to run out of the room and never audition again. But there I was, still standing there, wondering why I wasn't running away. I took a few deep breaths, made myself vulnerable, and just went for it. I couldn't let my 'what if' thoughts stand in the way of this meaningful audition. It's an opportunity of a lifetime; now I'm just praying for a call back. Fingers crossed!

COMEDY

BURPING

Look you're my little sister and I love you like crazy, and I know I give you big compliments – like, 'Good one, that was the best one yet,' or 'Come on, you can do better.' But now, I feel like I've created a monster by enabling you to keep doing it. It's hard to enjoy my food when you're rocketing off Godzilla burps at the kitchen table. It's impolite while we're eating, I feel like if I don't remind you, it's going to become a bad habit and then you'll just do it without even thinking about it. So, today is the day that you need to hear it: for future – you, you don't ever want to do this in front of your significant other, because if you do, the relationship won't stand a chance. OK, look – since we're not at the dinner table anymore, and you're far off from having a significant other, show me what you got.

DRAMATIC

GIZZY

I saw the sweetest little Scottish Terrier at the pet store last night with thick black hair, big dark eyes, and super short legs – just so cute! I already had his name picked out; I started calling him Gizzy, after my late grandpa. When I picked Gizzy up to cuddle with him, I was hooked; there was no way I was putting him back in that cage. I asked the employee how much he was. She was like, 'Oh, he's $500 off his total price, so he's only $4,000.' My mom and I looked at one another as if the building had just collapsed. They were asking way too much money, so we knew that getting him wasn't going to happen, and it broke my heart. As we were walking out to our car, the store manager followed us outside and apologized for the price mix up. It turned out that Gizzy was not $500 off – he was only $500 total! The manager said that he was aging out and needed to let him go. They were practically giving him away. We couldn't get back in there fast enough! After completing the paperwork, we got to take him home. He's already found his forever spot on the couch. We just love him.

DRAMATIC

I LOVE THE EIGHTIES

My grandma keeps telling me that being a teenager in today's world is way different from when she was a teen. Everything was more simple back in her day. They had cooler cars like Camaro, Trans Am, Z28, Chevelle Super Sport, and how everyone wishes they still had them today, since they would be worth a fortune; they also had phones that hung on the wall with a cord that could stretch all the way down the hall into another room. The clothes were way cooler: checkered bandanas, leg warmers, parachute pants, and Members Only jackets. Apparently, Grandma lost hers, but she has pictures. When she listened to her favorite bands it was on cassette tapes; she would pop it into a cassette player and hoped that the tape didn't get tangled when rewinding to hear her favorite song again. When that did happen, she had to use a pencil eraser to wind the tape back into the cassette case; that part sounded a little frustrating. I can only imagine what those times were like. My grandma said, if there were a tunnel that could take her back into the 80s, she would take me and go every other weekend.

COMEDY

PARENTS

Parents are so funny when they want to be. They try and pretend they don't care so we think they're cool, but deep down they care way too much. They can't fake this stuff. The other day, I pretended to argue with one of my friends on the phone, just to see my mom's reaction. I have to admit, she did a great job hiding her emotions – at first, anyway. Then, 321… My mom knocked on my bedroom door; she wanted to know if I had any laundry that needed washing. I asked her if she was OK. She nodded and was like, "Oh yeah, I'm good. Just doing laundry and thought you may need me to throw something in the wash for you." I gave her some clothes, said, Thank you, and right when the door was closing behind me, I noticed that she was still standing in the same spot. She looked over at me and said, "OK, I confess. I overheard you talking to your friend on the phone and wanted to say I thought you handled yourself very well. That's it. I'm off to do the laundry now." All I was thinking was, whoever's mother that is, I like her a lot. She didn't even ask questions.

COMEDY

THE LAKEHOUSE

We're all going to the lake house; you should go with us. I think we could all use a little getaway for the weekend. Don't you think? What do you mean, Jason lives there? Well, if he does, it was a long time ago, like way back in the '80s, he's probably too old to chase anyone now, just go with us. You'll have a nice time. We have a rope swing, jet skis, and lots of food for grilling out, not to mention the amazing view. It's awesome! Oh, you were serious? You watch way too many 80s horror movies! For the last time, Jason is not going to be at our lake house. It was just a movie; he was never real to begin with! Plus, there's going to be about 15 other people there, Jason can't get us all! Ok, I'll tell you what, forget the lake house. We can just grill out in my backyard, put up a tent, and pretend that we're camping instead.

COMEDY

MOVIE THEATER POPCORN

I probably wouldn't even go to the movies if it weren't for the hot, salty popcorn. But honestly, it's crazy how much a large bucket costs – it's nearly $10. It's ridiculous. I mean, the free refills do make it a better deal, so I can't complain too much. Come to think of it, does anyone really eat all of their popcorn from the first bucket? Never mind. All I know is, once I take my seat and the trailers are playing, I'm a caveman in action. I have no popcorn-eating etiquette. All through the previews, I'm shoving handfuls of popcorn into my mouth, with most of it falling on my lap, the floor, in my shirt – just everywhere! I should be embarrassed, but I'm not. I do feel sorry for the cleanup crew after I leave my seat and the lights come on. I guess that's why they have those big sweepers ready to go. They know what's up.

DRAMATIC

IT'S THE SIMPLE THINGS

I don't think people mean to be materialistic. No one is born to just want money and things; they learned that. To me, it's the simple things that really matter – you know, like when someone cooks for you or gives you a sweet note just to say they're thinking of you. Those mean something way more than material things. I think it's awesome to get to know one person so well that you can practically finish one another's sentences.

DRAMATIC

I SAW HER FIRST

This is not what good friends do. We can't go after the same girl; we look desperate and ridiculous. I mean, I get it. Look at her – she's beautiful. I bet she doesn't even look at us the same way we look at her; she can get anyone she wants, but I'm hoping she wants me. Let's get serious for just a minute here: her and I share a lot of things in common. For one, she likes horror movies, pizza on a Friday night, long phone chats, anime – you know stuff like that. You don't even like horror movies, so that cancels you out automatically. Look, I'm asking her out. I saw her first, and to be honest, I know this may be a longshot, but if the stars align, I'm going to marry this girl one day.

COMEDY

MOUTH OPEN

I went to Ally's to have dinner, but as soon as I got there, I was ready to leave. It was all I could do to not say anything. I even avoided striking up a conversation just so she wouldn't have to answer me. I know it seems shallow, but every time she spoke, all I could see was chewed-up food in her mouth. I was dodging food particles by the second; it would have made my night better had she just held up a napkin or something while she was eating and talking at the same time. I personally think it's presumptuous of her to think that I wouldn't be grossed out by that. I know I'm being a total jerk about this, and maybe I should have just told her how I felt about stuff like that, but I don't think it's my job to teach her those things. I just want to find a girl that has some natural table etiquette.

COMEDY

AND CUT!

It was amazing to be cast in the biggest movie of the year. It was even fine that I was not the main actor; I was just happy to be a part of a wonderful experience. Everyone was so nice and accommodating on the set; they kept making sure I was eating enough and staying hydrated. I had one line in the scene, and they were treating me as if I were the bee's knees. As soon as they yelled "action," I said my line loud and proud: "Give me back my coloring book and crayons Mr. Frog!" But then, all of a sudden, the Director yelled, "Cut," and we all froze. I was sure it wasn't me that caused the cameras to stop rolling, but apparently, it was. It turned out that I had the wrong line the whole time. I knew something was off – how many high school kids have a line that reads, "Give me back my coloring book and crayons, Mr. Frog?" The hard part was watching this little six-year-old cry his eyes out because I stole his only line. It was pretty humiliating. Thank God for lollipops, because when I gave him one, that made me a hero for the rest of the day.

DRAMATIC

PART-TIME JOB

I'm working a dead-end job. Every time I go into work, I'm already ready to leave. It doesn't pay very well, and it slows me way down on my creative studies. When I'm at work, all I hear is how someone needs more hours. I feel bad for them, so I'm more than happy to just give them mine, since I don't want to be there anyway. They don't seem to mind the busboy grind, like I do; some even have kids already and need to keep this job to put food on the table. I respect it, I really do, but I just started college, and I just can't put too much on my plate right now. Because being in the restaurant business isn't just about serving customers – you find yourself getting personal with others regarding their lives outside of work, and I have no time for that right now. So, I'm putting in my two weeks' notice.

DRAMATIC

WORRYING ABOUT THE FUTURE

I worry about everything and have lots of anxiety from it. Most of all I stress out about the future – I know that it won't make things better, but for some reason I do it anyway. Someone once told me that I have lots of depth and that's why I feel things so deeply. I just care about my family and hate to see them struggle. My grandmother, who's in her 50s, still works hard every day. She's always saying, "One day when I get all of my bills paid off, I'm going to quit my job and spend more time with you kids." Then, something happens – like she needs a new air conditioner or tires for her car – which makes her have to work more hours. I wish she could just chill out and hang with us more; I feel like she's missing out on our lives. I know, here I am thinking deeply again. I'm making it sound worse than it is. She's actually coming over this weekend and we're all having dinner together. I'm just overreacting.

DRAMATIC

VAPING CIRCLE

My friends are wanting to hang out tonight. I already know what they want to do: vape. They think it's so cool to Vape; it's become their new sneaky thing to do without anyone knowing, except our small friend group. I don't even feel inspired to hang out with them, since it's just going to be another "vape night" at the park. I feel for my friends, because instead of finding their creativity and making something more meaningful happen with their lives, they would rather vape it up, have a few laughs, then go home and start gaming until the sun comes up – then do it all over again the next night. I need to feel more inspired and make things happen in my life, but I don't want to let my friends down either. I guess it's time to start looking for clever excuses on why I can't hang out; it's just not my thing.

DRAMATIC

SMALL SACRIFICE

I don't understand. Were you just going to drop out of school like that and not tell us? You're going about this all wrong; you can't run away from your problems. You can have a baby without dropping out of school. I mean, it's not common, but it's not unheard of either. It doesn't matter what other people think; it's none of their business. In five years, none of this will even matter, so just finish. One day, when your baby is older, you'll look back on all of this and be glad you did. You'll be the best student and mom ever. Everyone will respect you more for how you handled the situation by pushing forward and following through with your goals. You're going to do great things.

DRAMATIC

NOSE RING

I was thinking about getting a nose ring – not a big one, though. What do you think? I've always wanted to do it; I just never had the nerve to go for it. I feel like if I get one, it'll look cool – like a small diamond or something. Nothing too crazy, just enough to turn heads and maybe even get a compliment or two. I was planning on going after school. If you go with me, you can help me pick it out. On second thought, maybe it's a bad idea. I heard that once you put a hole in your nose, it never closes up fully. I could just get the fake ones that stick on; that way I can take them off anytime, and I don't have to worry about a potential infection. Yeah, I think I'll do that instead. Wow, I just totally talked myself right out of getting a nose ring.

DRAMATIC

DREAMER

I have to take some chances if I want to succeed in life. It all starts with a dream, because without them, we have nothing to grab onto. Dreams can come true if we work hard and believe that they can happen. Some people just sit around thinking about them in hopes that someone will knock on the door and hand them their dreams on a silver platter without any effort at all, but it just doesn't happen that way – at least not in my world. It's not too late to dream; sometimes it's better late than never. We could be one of the lucky ones, as long as we don't lose our way.

DRAMATIC

JUST A FEELING

If you want to impress her, don't talk about your ex – bad move. She'll run for the hills. Breakups aren't easy, but she was obviously not the right girl for you. If she was, she wouldn't have run off with that soccer jock over an artist with entrepreneurial goals. I'm just being honest. The brunette that works at the trampoline place seems pretty nice. I heard she loves theme parks and horror movies – kind of like you! I don't know, she seems pretty cool, not to mention that she has a great sense of humor and laughs out loud when someone cracks a joke. Did I mention that she's single? I don't know, it could be a good thing. What have you got to lose?

COMEDY

COLLEGE ROOMMATE

My toothpaste, dental floss and oatmeal cookies are all missing. I also can't seem to find my nail clippers, either; they were sitting on the sink just a few minutes ago. Look, I'm not trying to accuse you of stealing my missing items, but you are the only person that I share a dorm with. I don't mind if you use my stuff, but you should ask me first. Wait, these are my brand-new shoes! Why do my shoelaces look like they went through a meat grinder? What's going on here? Whoa, when did we get a cat? Well, this explains everything!

DRAMATIC

CARLY

I was standing at the school entrance this morning when Carly walked over and asked me to sit with her and her friends at lunch today. I said, 'Yeah sure, I can do that.' We both smiled at one another; then the bell rang, so we had to rush off to class. At lunch, she scooted over to make room for me, but then she got up to take a call and walked off as if I didn't even exist anymore. Her friend told me that she was talking to her boyfriend, 'boyfriend?' I asked. Well, that would've been useful information this morning. Somehow that bothered me, but I let it roll off my shoulders and went to class. Is it too much to ask to just have a normal relationship with a person that isn't already taken? Later that day, I was told that she broke up with him and that's why she walked off; for some reason, that made me feel so much better.

DRAMATIC

LET THEM GO

It's hard when you like someone, and you're spending a lot of time with them, then this special someone, decides they don't want a relationship with you anymore. They don't want to be tied down, or they're thinking about the person before you and start comparing personality traits. But you've invested so much of your time and energy loving this person and helping them cope with their insecurities, just to find out, they're still insecure, and now they want to leave. Here you are feeling unsatisfied, unrewarded, isolated and empty. You're asking yourself, what just happened? You're always waiting for that next text from them hoping that they had a change of heart, you keep looking at your phone to see if their name lights up. Your emotional energy becomes drained, it messes you up psychologically and you feel as though you're the blame for the failure of the relationship. But I'm here to tell you, you're not to blame, they were just weak, they probably couldn't handle the reality of a strong independent person with depth, just let them go, they are not worth another minute of your time.

COMEDY

GEEK

I can't just ask her out; she's the most popular girl in school. There is no way she'll go out with me. But you're right – I have just as much of a chance as anyone else. The only problem is she only seems to go out with guys that look like Ken dolls, who drive expensive cars paid for by their parents, and live in big, rich houses. They probably can't even do basic math! I wouldn't even know how to take her out. I don't even have a car yet; I'm still riding my bike, for goodness sake. It's embarrassing, but I will have a good job one day and I will be CEO of my own company. Look at me: I'm a true geek, but I'm okay with that because I've got skills. I'm smart, creative and I'm a loving guy. She'll see it one day, and when she does, she'll find me more attractive and want to marry me. Maybe not today or tomorrow, but us geeks always win in the end. For now, I'm going to get busy increasing my confidence, one building block at a time – geek style.

DRAMATIC

SOMETHING NEW

I finally got my hair cut yesterday. After several years of not trimming it, all I know is I can finally see what's in front of me. Having long hair was just too much to manage; it became less cool and more annoying. I needed a change. I can always grow it back, if I miss it. I also decided to go back to my natural color. I was tired of the blonde streak – it didn't really fit my personality. You know, my friends are always telling me how lucky I am to have naturally dark hair, so I figured, why ruin a good thing? I have to admit that this haircut allows me to feel free. It's like I have more energy. It's weird. The only issue I'm having now is deciding which product to put in my hair without making it too sticky or stiff. I don't want it to look greasy or wet; I just want a subtle hold – something natural, and new. I could use some suggestions. Geez, I sound like I'm doing a commercial!

DRAMATIC

AGORAPHOBIA

I was scrolling through the channels on TV last night and found this new movie in the drama section that I thought looked pretty interesting. It's a "boy meets girl and falls in love" kind of story, except in this one, the girl can't leave her house because she has agoraphobia. Not sure why this grabbed my attention, but I had to see how it was going to end, so I was glued. It's heartbreaking to watch someone with so much anxiety – to the point where they're unable to leave their own homes without feeling like they're going to just die. I really hope I never get this way. I can only do so much indoors before I get bored; in the middle of the movie, I got a little anxious from feeling so bad for the girl that I was almost hyperventilating myself. I had to go outside for some fresh air to snap out of it. Although the story had me a bit on edge, it was definitely worth watching. Okay, so there's no spoiler alert here, but I feel like I should warn you: grab your tissues. It's a tearjerker.

DRAMATIC

I HEARD SOMETHING

I need to talk to you. I heard something today at the mall. I was sitting at the food court, minding my own business, when I overheard a bunch of girls from school talking about you. Do you remember that girl that you met at Johnny's party the other night? Well, she's only going out with you to make Brock the jock jealous. She's still in love with him, but he treats her with disrespect, so she's going out with you to show him that other guys find her desirable. It's pretty serious; please don't go out with her. It's just going to be humiliating. I've been your best friend since grade school. I feel like I can tell you anything, so I'm telling you now: she doesn't deserve you, and you're just going to get hurt.

DRAMATIC

EASILY OFFENDED

We live in a country where everyone seems to get easily offended; it's just too much to deal with. I know we can all be a bit sensitive at times, but some people just take everything too personally when it's really just us having different viewpoints, nothing more. In a perfect world, everyone would just be helping one another – no bullying, no complaining, no harsh words, no manipulating – just in it for the greater good. You know, I could go on and on, but basically, everyone would just be cool without being confrontational about things. I love the saying, "Let's just agree to disagree." It seems to work, for some. Anyway, I'm not sure where everything is headed, but I can't keep walking on eggshells like this. It's not healthy.

COMEDY

DOG TRICKS

My family was told by the Veterinarian that our dog is considered a senior now that he's seven years old, and that he may not feel like doing tricks anymore. Ever since that visit to the vet, it's like our dog could hear and understand everything that was said; now, he refuses to do even the slightest tricks for us. Every time I ask for his paw, he just sits and stares at me, like I'm crazy; after all of these years of training, he's just throwing in the towel. But as soon as I say the magic word 'treat,' he rolls over like he's putting out a fire. He even stands on his hind legs and walks all the way to the other side of the kitchen floor, as if he were belly dancing. I think my dog is actually playing tricks on me because now he refuses to do anything without a treat in my hand. I'm pretty sure that if my dog could talk, he would have a gangster tone while demanding that I hand over the whole box of treats – or else!

DRAMATIC

WEDDING BELLS

Just a few days ago, I didn't even want to care about Marty anymore. He's just stupid. If he can't see how much I like him, then I'm just going to start ignoring him. It's not what I want, but what else can I do? I'm a good catch; I'm the full package and he's... well, he's just dumb. But right when I thought he didn't even know I existed, he showed up at my locker yesterday and asked me if I had an extra pencil for history class. I swear, it was at that moment when our eyes locked together that I started planning our wedding. I even had the invitations with flowery prints picked out! The smile he gave me as he said, "thank you," was more than I could handle. I don't want him to know how I'll fly to the moon and back for him just yet, so I have to play a little hard to get, or I will look desperate. On second thought, who cares about that nonsense? I'm all in – wedding bells and all!

DRAMATIC

I THOUGHT WE WERE FRIENDS

We're all noticing that you've been really wrapped up in yourself lately. Every time we call to get together, you're always giving us an excuse on why you can't hang out. I thought we were friends – best friends! We're just not used to you giving us all of these weird reasons why you can't come around. So, if you have something going on that means more to you right now, just tell us; I'm sure we'll all understand. Your excuses lately are just not very good – like stubbing your toe and not being able to get your shoe on? Really? It's me you're talking to. Wild horses couldn't stop you from doing what you truly wanted to do, not even a stubbed toe. So, what gives?

SCENES

WE NEED TO DE-DORK YOU

Travis: Look, we really need to de-dork you.

Brian: De-dork me? Why?

Travis: Yes! Every time a girl walks up to you, you stop talking and start staring at her eyebrows.

Brian: Is that bad?

Travis: Really? Yeah, that's bad. You have to have a conversation, you know? Learn how to talk to her about things, like sports. Okay, maybe not sports right off the bat… maybe her favorite pet, or food, a favorite travel place. Anything!

Brian: But what if she rolls her eyes and walks off?

Travis: Why would she roll her eyes?

Brian: You know, because I might say something in 'dork language.'

Travis: "Dork language?" Ha! That's funny. Look, all kidding aside, you have to reach deep down inside, find your confidence and go for it.

Brian: 'Confidence and go for it?' Is there a store for purchasing something like that?

Travis: I'm serious – if she rolls her eyes and walks off, then she's not the one. You've got charm. You're funny, don't be afraid to show it.

Brian: What if she's the one, but I say something stupid and then she thinks I'm a dork, too?

Travis: If she walks away without looking twice, then she might not be interested. But if she gives you a grin while looking back at you, that could be a good start to something more. You never know.

Brian: Good point.

Travis: Just be yourself.

Brian: Okay, next time I see her, I'm going to ask her if she likes gardening.

Travis: Gardening? What?

Brian: I mean, who doesn't like gardening; it's cool to grow your own food.

Travis: Brian, when have you ever planted anything?

Brian: Don't you remember a few years ago? I planted pumpkin seeds. That counts, doesn't it?

Travis: Yeah, but they never grew.

Brian: That's not the point! I can't help it that the rain flooded my seeds back out.

Travis: Maybe you could start with something simpler and cute, like her favorite pet. Most girls love puppies and kittens.

Brian: True.

Travis: The conversations are endless when pets are involved.

Brian: That's it! I'm buying a puppy. I gotta go. Thanks, for the encouragement.

GOOD FRIENDS

Blain: Are you going to ask Kimberly out?

Tommy: I don't know yet; I'm thinking about it. Why?

Blain: She's hot. I mean she's not *just* hot, she's super smart.

Tommy: I've known her for a long time; we're just good friends.

Blain: I don't want to step on any toes here, but…

Tommy: What do you mean?

Blain: Either you ask her out, or I will.

Tommy: I'm just taking things slow. I don't want to ruin a good friendship between us.

Blain: If you wait too long, she'll think you're not interested and start dating someone else – like me.

Tommy: Really?

Blain: Look, life is now. If you like her, go for it!

Tommy: What if she doesn't like me back?

Blain: I see the way she looks at you. She's interested; I would bet on it.

Tommy: How much?

Blain: Nothing. I would lose; she likes you. Go for it!

Tommy: I'm not sure what to say. I just don't want to ruin what we have.

Blain: Just tell her how you feel – unless you're just not interested. But if you don't, someone else will.

Tommy: True.

Blain: What are you afraid of?

Tommy: I don't know. Maybe not doing things right.

Blain: We're all afraid of that, but so what? You've gotta try, or you'll never know.

Tommy: Yeah, you're right.

Blain: That's right. I'm right. Now, go for it before we both turn 100 yrs. old!

Tommy: I need to figure out what I'm going to say.

Blain: Okay, ready? Kimberly, you're one of my best friends, but it's time to shift gears here. We've known each other a long time. It's no secret that we both desire to be more than friends.

Tommy: Desire?

Blain: You know what I mean.

Tommy: What if –

Blain: What if what? Go be her boyfriend and just have fun together!

Tommy: Maybe you're right. Okay, I'll let you know what happens.

Blain: I'll be waiting with open ears.

I KNOW YOU

Chris: Hey, I'm Chris from the coffee shop on Pine Forest.

Kelly: I knew you looked familiar.

Chris: I've made your espresso latte's a few times.

Kelly: Oh yeah, I thought I recognized you. How do you like working there?

Chris: It's pretty cool. I get to meet a lot of people and, of course, try all the new holiday coffees when we get them.

Kelly: That's awesome. Which one is your favorite?

Chris: The Peppermint Loco Mocha is pretty good. They put a real peppermint stick in it, so after your done with the drink, you get to hang on to the peppermint taste for a while longer.

Kelly: That sounds good. Next time I come in I would love to try it.

Chris: Cool, just let me know and I'll make it for you.

Kelly: It's kind of weird – I never drink coffee at home, only when I go to coffee shops.

Chris: Same. There's something about the atmosphere and smell of coffee in the air. I'm addicted.

Kelly: I totally get it. It has that effect on me, too.

Chris: Where do you work?

Kelly: I work at the theater on Bay Street. Once I get out of school, I go straight to work.

Chris: I go there with my friends all the time, but I don't remember seeing you there.

Kelly: That's because every time you walk in, I go in the other room.

Chris: Why?

Kelly: I don't know. I think I just get a little embarrassed.

Chris: Embarrassed?

Kelly: I just feel like after being there all day, I'm covered in butter and salt from the popcorn, and it makes me feel gross. I don't want you to see me like that.

Chris: I get that; I would probably feel the same way. But that doesn't change how pretty you are.

Kelly: You think I'm pretty?

Chris: I always thought you were pretty.

Kelly: I didn't even know you knew me.

Chris: You've been on my mind, since making your third espresso latte, I just never said anything.

Kelly: I never knew that; why didn't you say anything?

Chris: I was afraid of saying something stupid.

Kelly: I'm always saying something stupid.

Chris: I don't believe that for a second.

Kelly: Trust me, I do.

Chris: Oh, well, should I be worried?

Kelly: Yes – no, I mean, I don't know.

CHICKEN SOUP FOR MY BROTHER

Mark: Who are you? And what did you do with my sister?

Sam: Ha-ha, very funny.

Mark: I'm serious. What are you doing?

Sam: I'm making Chicken Noodle soup.

Mark: Homemade?

Sam: That's right.

Mark: Now I know you're an imposter. Who are you, and what did you do with Sam?

Sam: So, you don't want it?

Mark: Is it really homemade?

Sam: Maybe. Why? Would that make you like it better?

Mark: Yeah, it would.

Sam: What do you consider homemade?

Mark: I don't know. Natural ingredients, something like that.

Sam: Then yes, it's homemade.

Mark: You're cooking me homemade Chicken Noodle soup? Did you hit your head or something?

Sam: Ha, very funny. Come to think of it, I did bump my head on the table this morning, but I'm good.

Mark: I knew it.

Sam: What do you mean?

Mark: In case you forgot, you hate cooking. You won't even make a peanut butter and jelly sandwich.

Sam: It's Saturday, I had nothing better to do.

Mark: It's Sunday, I'm sure you could find something better to do.

Sam: Mom said you were sick, so I figured I would make you some soup because I'm not trying to get sick.

Mark: Oh, I see. You're scared I'm contagious and that I'm going to pass it on to you? (opens garbage to throw his Kleenex away, then notices a soup box.)

Sam: Well, don't look too surprised.

Mark: Oh, did I look surprised? I don't think I looked surprised.

Sam: Ok, you caught me, but technically packaged soup is homemade. I just didn't make it myself, but I did use two cups of filtered water, so… *voila*!

Mark: "Voila?"

Sam: Yeah, it means, 'there it is!' What did you expect? I'm not a chef, you know. I just wanted you to feel better.

Mark: How hard did you actually bump your head on the table this morning?

Sam: Just eat it. It's good.

Mark: I'm just giving you a hard time, but you did say it was homemade.

Sam: There's no way, it takes way too long to prepare.

Mark: When you get sick with a cold, I'll just make you packaged soup too. How about that?

Sam: Sounds perfect to me.

Mark: Really? Well, as far as I am concerned that brand you used has no nutritional value.

Sam: When I'm sick, I'm not picky. Also, how would you even know?

Mark: Whatever, I guess. And I know because that brand you have, is full of chemicals!

Sam: Yeah, and?

Mark: And, if you look on the back, you will see why it's bad. I can't eat this; I'll feel worse.

Sam: Are you kidding me? I have things I need to…

Mark: Ouch, my body. My temperature is increasing (pretend agony).

Sam: Seriously?

Mark: I'm serious. The pain is getting so bad, it's making me send mom that picture of you and Johnny.

Sam: You wouldn't dare!

Mark: Try me. However, there is a way to escape this tragic scenario, but it seems you're already aware of that. So, in that case, I guess I'll press se …

Sam: Ugh, fine. Where do we keep the ingredients, anyway?

MOVIE TIME

Christy: Glad you could join me.

Katie: What do you mean?

Christy: Every time we come to the movies, you're always late.

Katie: That's because I want to look my best. It takes me a minute.

Christy: It's dark, it's not like anyone can see you.

Katie: That's not true. I was just buying popcorn and ran into a few of my parents' friends. I even got a compliment on my shirt.

Christy: Well, at least you got the popcorn. And yeah, that shirt is pretty nice.

Katie: That's right, so calm down.

Christy: Oh, we've got to see this one!

Katie: Yeah, I know. I saw this trailer the last time we were here. We definitely have to see this one.

Christy: Hey, isn't that Mike Wood over there in the front row with John's girlfriend, Lisa?

Katie: Oh shoot, I think it is. But I heard they broke up, so it's fair game.

Christy: Dang, they didn't waste any time hooking up.

Katie: I know. It just goes to show how there's always someone lurking around the corner to take your place.

Christy: I guess so. That's crazy.

Katie: I agree, it is crazy. I think it's too soon, but they obviously don't think so.

Christy: Obviously. It's only been a week – I guess a week could be long enough.

Katie: They dated for two years! One week seems like a slap in the face.

Christy: Yeah, true. That's not long enough to forget about someone after that many years of dating. That's definitely a slap in the face.

Katie: Oh well, we can't worry about it. It's their lives. But what's up with this long trailer? Doesn't it seem like we just watched most of the movie?

Christy: I was thinking the same thing. Had they just added an ending, that would've been it – movie over! Finally, the actual movie is starting.

Katie: About time!

Christy: Don't look now, but is that John?

Katie: Yes! Oh my gosh, how is he here at the same time as Mike?

Christy: This has to be a coincidence; there's no way they planned this.

Katie: How can we watch the movie on the screen when there's actual real drama in the room?

Christy: Let's just ignore them; pretend they're not here.

Katie: Look at John's face. He doesn't look happy.

Christy: Mike looks like he's super happy – he just put his arm around Lisa!

Katie: Shhh – the movie is on; we have to ignore them.

Christy: Oh no, John is walking toward the first row.

Katie: Give me the popcorn.

Christy: Here, just grab some. I need to hold it, just in case.

Katie: Just in case what?

Christy: You know – look!

Katie: Oh my gosh, did John just pour popcorn all over Mike's head?

Christy: Oh yeah, this is getting real!

Katie: Sure is. Now everyone's yelling at them to be quiet.

Christy: Save me some popcorn.

Katie: Here.

Christy: We're actually missing our movie.

Katie: That's Ok, this one is much better!

Christy: Oh my gosh!

Katie: Holy fight! This is intense.

Christy: Dang, the manager is breaking it up.

Katie: What do you mean? Someone was about to get seriously hurt.

Christy: Yeah, I know.

Katie: Ok, I think you actually enjoyed that.

Christy: Ugh, maybe a little bit.

Katie: Yeah, I think I did too.

Christy: Now that the live drama is over, we just missed the whole beginning of our movie.

Katie: Let's get a refund and come back tomorrow. Popcorn is gone anyway.

Christy: Yeah, let's go. I've seen enough for one day. I have a feeling someone's going home unhappy right about now.

Katie: No doubt about it.

FRESH AIR

Jenna: Excuse me, do you have a cigarette?

Finn: What?

Jenna: Do you have a cigarette?

Finn: No, do I look like I smoke?

Jenna: Kind of.

Finn: What do people look like that smoke?

Jenna: I don't know – the ones that look preppy, like you. Are you sure you don't have a cigarette on you?

Finn: Well, I don't consider myself preppy, but like I said, I don't smoke. You'll have to ask someone else.

Jenna: Why not?

Finn: Why not what?

Jenna: Why don't you smoke?

Finn: Because it's unhealthy and smells bad.

Jenna: Ok then, relax. Geez.

Finn: Why do *you* smoke?

Jenna: I don't. Just socially when I go out with friends.

Finn: Do you always ask strangers for cigarettes?

Jenna: Well, that's the thing – I don't. You're my first. I know they're not healthy for me. Anyway, it's all good; I'm just a little stressed out.

Finn: What are you stressed out about? And why are you standing outside the restaurant? It's pretty cold out here tonight.

Jenna: My friends are inside, and one slipped up and blurted out that she was in love with my ex-boyfriend. I mean, not that it matters, because it doesn't. He is my ex, and I shouldn't be upset about it, but for some reason, it bothers me. She's supposed to be one of my closest friends. Anyway, I decided to just come outside for some fresh air and think about things for a minute. Then I saw you standing here and thought if you had a cigarette, I would smoke it.

Finn: I don't blame you for being upset. That's a pretty crappy thing to do to someone. So, you came out to get fresh air, but then you wanted to smoke?

Jenna: Yeah, I know, it makes no sense. It's just me having an upset moment, and cigarettes seem like a good rebellious thing to do when I'm feeling unhappy. Nothing more.

Finn: I'm Finn.

Jenna: Hi, I'm Jenna.

Finn: You look familiar.

Jenna: I come here with my parents sometimes.

Finn: Yeah, I've seen you.

Jenna: You look familiar also, do you eat here often?

Finn: A lot, actually.

Jenna: They have really good burgers here.

Finn: I know.

Jenna: Are you here with someone?

Finn: I guess you can say that; my parents own this place.

Jenna: That's awesome! Now I know why you look familiar – I've seen you here.

Finn: So, this may sound crazy, I know we just met, but we should hang out sometime.

Jenna: No crazier than me asking you for a cigarette. I would like that.

Finn: Cool. I hope you're not tired of eating burgers.

Jenna: I love burgers.

Finn: Still want a cigarette?

Jenna: No thanks, just the burger and maybe a shake.

Finn: Well, I just happen to know a great place.

Jenna: Yeah, me too.

POLKA-DOT-DRESS

Laurie: Hey Christine, how do I look?

Christine: Umm, great, but did you know that there's a lot of polka-dots on your dress? It's pretty interesting. Interesting. Did I say that already?

Laurie: Wait, what do you mean by interesting?

Christine: Oh, I'm sorry. I didn't mean to sound like I didn't like your dress. You look great.

Laurie: Yeah, I thought so too, but the polka-dots were like the very first thing that you commented on, which tells me they're a little too much. Are they?

Christine: Are they what?

Laurie: The Polka-Dots. Are they too much?

Christine: Ok, Laurie, I have to admit it: I really do like polka-dots, but just not on clothing. It just looks like you're trying too hard. I mean, it's working, but not like you think it is. It's just... well, it's just not working.

Laurie: Not working?

Christine: The polka-dots are a distraction, I mean, no one wears polka-dots, unless they're doing a sequel to Madagascar.

Laurie: Christine, polka-dots are my life! That's why my bed sheets and comforter have polka-dots on them. You know that.

Christine: Yes, I get it. And trust me I understand your love for polka-dots, like at home in your pajamas or something, but not in public.

Laurie: Great, Christine. I mean you're my best friend, but I can't help but feel a little hurt by your comments right now.

Christine: I'm sorry. I know I sound insensitive, but don't you want your best friend to be honest when something doesn't look good?

Laurie: Yes, of course I do. But it's your delivery that's making me upset. Do you know that there's a better way to get your point across without hurting my feelings?

Christine: Well, as your friend and secret-keeper, I just don't want anyone to say anything negative about your dress. That's all.

Laurie: I mean it doesn't look *that* bad… does it?

Christine: No, it doesn't look that bad. Look, I don't know. Don't listen to me.

Laurie: I guess I'll go and take it off now, since I will definitely not be wearing it out anywhere. Ever.

Christine: No need to get upset, Laurie. I thought we were supposed to be honest with one another about everything. Don't you remember calling me out on my flowery jumpsuit with the hole under the armpit area? It was my favorite, and you laughed out loud and told me there was no way I was going out dressed like that if I wanted to remain friends with you. I know you remember that.

Laurie: I do remember that – you were very upset about it – but that's beside the point. We're talking about my polka-dotted, horrible dress right now. I'm just a little disappointed because I thought it looked cool, nice.

Christine: Look, I have a great idea!

Laurie: I can only imagine. Well, let's hear it.

Christine: Close your eyes and picture this: let's make cool pillowcases with it. And I'm not being sarcastic; it would actually match perfectly with your comforter. Are you picturing it?

Laurie: Maybe. I mean, I suppose that would work. The only problem is, I can't sew.

Christine: Okay, hand it to me. By tomorrow afternoon, you will have two beautiful polka-dotted pillowcases. You're welcome.

DAMIANO'S ON FAIRFAX

First Actor: Are you hungry?

Second Actor: Always!

First Actor: Let's go to Damiano's for some spaghetti and cream soda.

Second Actor: I'm all about that place. I haven't been there in so long. Is it still down on Fairfax Avenue?

First Actor: I sure hope so. It's been a while.

Second Actor: Wow, that place is so nostalgic to me.

First Actor: I remember the kitchen being right next to the entrance; you could see the chef putting in the spaghetti while stirring the sauce as you walked in. It would make my mouth water every time.

First Actor: Oh yeah, that's right; I don't know if everything's the same, but I once loved the ambient lighting in that place. I wonder if they still have the red, round glass candles sitting at the booths. I remember how conversations were just more fun when the lights were dimmed – it was like a vibe, you know?

Second Actor: Totally true. That place was like a hidden gem; they were always known for having the best Italian food.

First Actor: I know, their spaghetti was like finding gold. It was made al dente, and the sauce was kind of sweet, but you could definitely taste the basil.

Second Actor: My mouth is watering so much right now just thinking about it.

First Actor: Same! Why are we still sitting here?

Second Actor: I don't know. I was just thinking the same thing.

First Actor: Come on, I'll drive.

Second Actor: Let's go.

First Actor: Wait! What if it's not there anymore?

Second Actor: I sure hope it is, because my taste buds couldn't take the rejection right now.

First Actor: Mine can't either.

Second Actor: We should just call and find out.

First Actor: Here, I'll call. Hi! Since you answered the phone saying, 'Damiano's' that tells me that you guys are still there after all of these years. Really? Oh, that's great! Thank you. We'll see you soon.

Second Actor: This is exciting! Nostalgia, here we come!

ABOUT THE AUTHOR

KeriAnne Dawson has been a member of The Screen Actors Guild (SAG) and The American Federation of Television and Radio Artists (AFTRA) – now unified as SAG-AFTRA – since 1993. She possesses extensive acting experience spanning both stage and screen.

Beyond her performances, KeriAnne is dedicated to nurturing new talent through directing children's workshops and musical cabarets; she finds great reward in teaching aspiring actors the essential skills needed to develop characters within given circumstances, ensuring they perform with a deep understanding of character and reality.

Designed for the next generation of performers, this book for teens features 59 original monologues and eight short scenes. These materials assist young actors with auditions and performances, or simply provide a fun way to practice with friends.

KeriAnne believes that learning builds confidence necessary for actors to express their own unique voices and build compelling characters. Having appeared in numerous commercials, television shows, and films, she has now found her place writing monologues and scenes for students to practice their craft.

www.ingramcontent.com/pod-product-compliance
Lightning Source LLC
LaVergne TN
LVHW010455160826
845677LV00012B/2490

* 9 7 9 8 2 1 8 8 9 2 8 9 0 *